25 Delicious Salad Recipes Cookbook

Alex John

TERMS & CONDITIONS

TABLE OF CONTENTS

Introduction

Salads are super duper delicious. Don't you agree? Not only they are delicious but are also healthy. Now you might have heard Tony Robins stressing on the fact that one should include salads in his diet. It also detoxifies your body and keeps it fresh from into. Don't believe me? Try out the recipes given in this book and tell me later on. ☺

This book contains awesome recipes that don't go hard on your pocket and will also leave you with a smile. Are you ready to check out the great

diversity of these salad recipes? So!!
Here we go!!

Awesome Avocado Salad

What you need:

- 1/4 to 1/2 teaspoon salt to taste
- 1 1/2 freshly sliced sweet onion
- Freshly ground black pepper to top
- 2 fresh avocados
- Fresh cilantro (Chopped)
- Juice of 1/2 or maybe 1lemon
- 1 Finely chopped bell pepper (Green)

What to do:

1. Take all the fresh ingredients. Wash them. Now take a mixing salad bowl. After that you should combine the peeled, pitted

and welldiced avocado, sliced sweet onion, chopped green bell pepper, and freshly shredded cilantro.

2. Then drizzle fresh lime juice of about 1/2 to 1 lemon.

3. For seasoning top salt to taste and add freshly ground black pepper.

4. Then flip them very well and serve them fresh and delicious.

Simple Blueberry Vinaigrette

What you need:

- 2 1/2 tsp lemon juice
- 2 Tbsps orange marmalade
- 1/4 cup vegetable oil
- 1/4 to half tsp salt
- 1 cup fresh or may be frozen blueberries, thawed (Divided)
- 1 to 2 teaspoon Dijon mustard

What to do:

1. Take a blender and in that blender, mix 1/2 of the blueberries with the other ingredients; blend until a smooth dressing forms.
2. Place the dressing into the salad and top it up with the left blueberries.

Yields: Servings: 4 to 5

Easy Celery And Onion Salad

What you need:

- 5 to 6 basil leaves
- 2 to 3 onions (Diced)
- Ground pepper, to taste
- 1 stalk celery(Shredded)
- Drizzle of olive oil
- 2 tablespoons. Lemon juice
- Pinch of salt

What to do:

1. Combinewhole the ingredients in a bowl and flip well till all the ingredients are mixed correctly.
2. Refrigerate and serve.

Awesome Fattoush

What you need:

- Flatbread, such as pita bread
- 2 1/2 large, ripe tomatoes, in bite size pieces
- pepper and sea salt
- 2 stalks fresh basil, roughly chopped
- Juice of 1 to 2 lemon
- 1/4 to 1/2 bunch fresh parsley, roughly chopped

<u>For the toasted bread:</u>

- 1/2 cucumber (Diced)
- Around 1/3 cup olive oil

What to do:

1. Blend the lemon juice with the tomatoes and cucumbers.
2. Combine the shredded herbs and toss to mix.
3. Dice the bread, put into a bowl, and top with olive oil.
4. Blend well so that all the pieces are wet with oil.
5. Place the bread on a baking sheet and toast in a preheated oven (320 to 330°F) for approximately 10 to 15 minutes, or maybe till crisp and golden.
6. Let the toasted bread cool slightly before mixing with the salad.

7. Sprinkle with sea salt and pepper and now you can serve.

Servings: 3 to 4

Superb Mango Salsa Salad

What you need:

- 1 sliced red bell paper
- 1 to 2 chopped green onion
- 1 fine sliced fresh jalapeno pepper
- 1 chopped mango
- 3 1/2 tbsp. of lemon juice
- 3 tbsp. freshly chopped cilantro

What to do:

1. Now wash the mango, peel and cut it.
2. Take a mixing bowl and then you should combine the mangos, shredded green onion,red bell pepper, freshly sliced cilantro and

finely sliced jalapeno pepper.
Mix them well.

3.   Cover the bowl and allow the
mixture to soak in the juices
for 30 to 40 minutes.

4.   Put this salsa out in a serving
dish and serve it with chips
or may be with fish.

Epic Red Onion And Spinach Salad

What you need:

- 1/2 cup Fresh Mozzarella cheese
- Oregano, to taste
- 3 to 4 cucumbers (Sliced)
- 1 to 1 1/2 bunch fresh baby spinachs
- Crumble some slice of bacon, if you desire (Optional)
- 2 red onions, finely shredded

What to do:

1. Combine all the ingredients, except for the cheese, in a bowl and flip well till all the ingredients are mixed thoroughly

2. After that refrigerate it and serve it by topping it with the cheese.

Yummy Tuna Salad

What you need:

- Capers, as per taste
- Pepper to taste
- 1 can of tuna
- Lime juice, as required
- 1 mashed avocado
- 2 tomatoes, finely chopped
- 1 to 2 scallion (Sliced)
- Salt to taste

What to do:

1. First of all, mash the avocado with a fork. Combine lime juice to it till it is smooth.

2. Now fold in the shredded tomatoes, drained tuna, capers and scallion into the mashed avocado.

3. Season with black pepper and add salt to taste.
4. Serve this delicious tuna salad with chips or may be with vegetables or maybe on a bed of greens.

Fantastic Warm Escarole, Egg & Pancetta Salad

What you need:

- 2 heads escarole, tough outer leaves removed, torn into bite sized pieces
- Salt and freshly ground pepper
- 1 to 2 clove garlic, bruised
- 1 to 1 1/2 tablespoon whole grain mustard
- 2 to 3 tbsp red wine vinegar, plus 1 teaspoon
- 4 pieces thick to now cut pancetta or bacon (Chopped)
- 4 large eggs
- 1/4 to 1/2 cup extra virgin olive oil

What to do:

1. If using bacon, bring a small saucepan of water to a boil. Add the bacon and simmer for 5 to 10 minutes to tame its smoky, salty flavor. Drain, shift to paper towels, and blot dry.

2. Then wipe out the saucepan, put above medium to low heated up, and now you should combine the oil, garlic, and pancetta or bacon. Cook, occasionally stirring, till the garlic is golden and the pancetta are crisp about 2 to 5 minutes.

3. You should be careful to not let the garlic burn. Remove

from the heat and discard the garlic. Stir in the mustard and the 2 tbsp vinegar. Set apart.

4. Choose a large, wide pan with a tight fitting lid. Fill with a generous amount of water and add one teaspoon vinegar, put over high heat, and bring to a rolling boil. Reduce the heating to a very gentle simmer.

5. Now working quickly, crack the eggs one at a time into a small bowl and then slide the eggs into the simmering water. Poach the eggs till the whites are set, and the yolks are still soft for 5 to 10

minutes. Meanwhile, bring the vinegar mixture to a boil.

6.   Place the escarole in a large bowl. Pour the vinegar mixture above the escarole and instantly toss to wilt the leaves slightly. Season with salt and pepper.

7.   Flip again and arrange on individual plates. Remove every poached egg with a slotted spoon, blot the bottom dry, and slide onto the salads.

8.   Season the eggs with salt and pepper and then you can serve.

Serves: 4 to 5

Fantastic Couscous Salad With Dried Cranberries & Roasted Chicken

What you need:

- 2 tbsp sherry vinegar
- 1 to 2 cup instant couscous
- 2 carrots, peeled and sliced
- 2 green onions, including green parts(Sliced)
- 1 tablespoon thinly sliced fresh mint
- 1/3 cup dried cranberries
- Salt and freshly ground pepper
- 2 cups sliced roasted chicken meat
- 1/2 to 1 cup extra virgin olive oil

What to do:

1. In a small saucepan, blend 1 1/2 cups water and teaspoon salt and boil them.

2. Stir in the couscous and continue boiling.

3. Remove from the flame, then cover it and let it stand for 5 to 10 minutes.

4. Transfer to a bowl and fluff with a fork to separate the grains.

5. Now you should combine the green onions, carrots, and dried cranberries.

6. In a small bowl, whisk together the vinegar and salt and pepper to taste.

7. Now you should add the oil in a thin stream, constantly

whisking till the dressing is smooth.

8.   Now pour over the couscous mixture and whisk to blend well.

9.   Shift the couscous to a serving dish and arrange the sliced chicken on top.

10.   Top with the mint and serve.

Serves: 4

Delicious Fruit Salad Bowl With Yogurt

What you need:

- 3 1/2 cups mixed berries of choice
- 3 tbsps honey
- A dash of cinnamon
- 2 cups yogurt
- 2 tablespoon orange zest
- 1 banana(Sliced)
- 1/2 orange juice
- 1 bunch grapes(Seedless)

What to do:

1. In a medium mixing bowl, add the honey and yogurt.
2. Inaclear bowl, mix the orange juice, banana, orange zest, grapes, and berries.

3. Stir with care to blend.
4. Divide fruit salad among serving bowls, sprinkle cinnamon on top and serve chilled.

Ready in about: 20 to 25 minutes

Serves: 6 to 7

Handsome Raw Quinoa And Veggie Salad

What you need:

- 4 plum tomatoes (Diced)
- 1 to 2 cup red quinoa
- 1/2 cup scallions, finely shredded
- 2 cloves garlic (Minced)
- 1 cucumber, peeled and thinly sliced
- 3 tablespoons extra virgin olive oil
- 4 cups water
- 1 cup fresh parsley (Sliced)
- 1/3 cup toasted almonds, coarsely sliced
- 8 dates, coarsely shredded
- 1 1/2 tsp salt
- 2 tbsps balsamic vinegar

- Juice of 1 fresh lemon
- 1/2 teaspoon celery seeds
- 1/4 teaspoon black pepper
- 1 to 2 tablespoon orange juice

What to do:

1. Bring water to a boil over high medium heat.
2. Reduce the heating and cook the quinoa for 15 to 20 minutes. Drain and set aside.
3. In a large bowl, combine the rest of things you need(i.e. ingredients)
4. Combine the quinoa and whisk to blend ingredients.

Ready in about: 20 to 25 minutes

Serves: 7 to 8

Cool Spinach Salad With Garlic Dressing

What you need:

<u>For the Salad:</u>

- 1/4 cup sun dried tomatoes
- 1 cup cooked spelt
- 2 hard boiled eggs (Sliced)
- 4 cups baby spinach
- 1/4 to 1/2 cup olives, pitted and halved

<u>For the Salad Dressing:</u>

- 1/2 to 1 teaspoon seasoned salt
- 1/4 cup canola oil
- 1/2 teaspoon sweet paprika
- 2 to 3 cloves garlic(Minced)
- 1 tablespoon molasses
- Juice of 1 fresh lemon
- 1/4 tsp black pepper

What to do:

1. In a large bowl, combine the spinach, tomatoes, spelt and olives.
2. In an electric blender or a food processor, blend dressing ingredients until smooth.
3. Taste and adjust seasonings.
4. Divide the salad among serving bowls; drizzle prepared garlic dressing and top with sliced egg.

Ready in about: 20 to 30 minutes

Serves: 3

Rocking Quinoa Salad With Avocado And Dried Fruits

What you need:

- 3 tablespoons olive oil
- 1 1/4 cups quinoa
- 1 to 2 teaspoon salt
- 3 1/2 tbsps golden raisins
- 3 tbsps dates, coarsely shredded
- 2 1/2 cups water
- 3 tablespoons orange juice
- 2 tablespoon orange zest
- 3 to 4 green onions, thinly sliced
- 1 tsp red pepper
- Black pepper to taste
- 1/4 cup pecans, coarsely chopped

- 2 medium ripe avocados, peeled and diced
- 1 1/2 tsp ground cumin

What to do:

1. Take a large saucepan and bring water, the quinoa, and sea salt to a boil.
2. Reduce the heat to low, and simmer for separate 10 to 15 minutes.
3. Combine the raisins and shredded dates. Cook 5 to 15 minutes more, until the liquid is absorbed.
4. Fluff the quinoa with a fork and now allow it to cool.
5. To prepare the dressing: follow 6 to 9

6. In another bowl, stir the orange juice, red pepper, orange zest, olive oil, cumin and black pepper.

7. In a different large bowl, blend quinoa mixture, dressing, avocado, green onions, and pecans. Taste and adjust the seasonings.

8. Now serve at room temperature.

Ready in about: 30 to 35 minutes

Servings: 6

Advanced Avocado Tuna Salad
What you need:

- 5 to 6 ounces cooked or may be canned wild tuna
- 1 to 2 lemon, juiced, to taste
- Low sodium salt and pepper to taste
- 1 avocado
- 1 cup chopped tomatoes
- 1 tablespoon chopped onion, to taste

What to do:

1. Cut the avocado in half and scoop the middle of both avocado halves into a bowl, leaving a shell of avocado flesh of about 1/4 inch thick on every half.
2. Now you should add lemon juice and onion to the

avocado in the bowl and mash them together.

3. Then combine tuna, lowsodiumpepper, and salt, and stir to mix.

4. Taste and adjust if needed.

5. Fill avocado shells with tuna salad and serve.

Excellent Chinese Salad

What you need:

Salad :

- 1/4 to 1 cup radishes (Julienned)
- 1 cup carrot julienned (about 1 large carrot)
- 1/4 cup scallions, trimmed and julienned (about 3 scallions)
- 2 cups cooked chicken or may be turkey
- 1 small head savoy cabbage, finely shredded
- 1/4 to 1/2 cup fresh cilantro (Shredded)
- 1/4 to 1/2 cup fresh mint (Shredded)

Vinaigrette:

- 1/2 to 1 tsp chili flakes
- Low sodium salt to taste
- Stevia to taste
- 2 tablespoons coconut or maybe rice vinegar
- 1 chipotle pepper
- 2 to 3 Tbsps sesame oil
- 1 1/2 tsp fresh ginger (Grated)
- 1 clove garlic (Crushed)

What to do:

1. Combine carrots, cabbage, radishes, and scallions.
2. Top with chicken, cilantro and mint and set apart.
3. Combine the vinaigrette.
4. Taste to see if it needs any adjustments.

5. If it is too spicy, you can combine more lime juice to counteract it.

6. Drizzle salad with vinaigrette & enjoy

Dashing Tuna Stuffed Tomato

What you need:

- 1/4 tsp. low sodium salt
- Lettuce leaves
- 1/4 to 1/2 tsp. ground black pepper
- 6 tbsp. olive oil and 1 tbsp rice vinegar
- 2 large tomatoes
- 1 stalk celery(Chopped)
- 1/2 to 1 small onion, cut
- 2 (5 to 6 oz.) cans wild albacore tuna

What to do:

1. First of all, wash and dry the tomatoes and remove any stem. You can either slice off the top part of the tomatoes

and hollow them out or cut every tomato into wedges, making sure only to cut down to approximately 1/2 an inch before you get to the bottom of the tomato.

2. Arrange the tomatoes on a plate on top of lettuce leaves.

3. Combine the remaining ingredients in a mixing bowl and combine additional low sodium salt and pepper if desired. Spoon into the tomatoes and serve.

Special Turkey Sprouts Salad

What you need:

- 1/2 white onion, finely diced
- 1/2 cup sliced almonds
- 1/2 pound of brussels sprouts
- 2 turkey breasts (Sliced)

Vinaigrette:

- Few grinds of black pepper
- 1 tbsp quality mustard powder
- 1 tablespoon avocado oil
- 2 to 3 tbsp Apple Cider Vinegar
- Stevia to taste
- 1/2 to 1 teaspoon low sodium salt

What to do:

1. Cut the brussels sprouts in half and thinly slice. Chop

the 1/2 cup of almonds. Finely dice the white onion. Scallions would work too if you prefer a more mild onion flavor though the white did not overpower.

2. Remove the breasts and chop into bite sized pieces. Combineall of these ingredients into a large bowl and then lightly flip the Brussels sprouts salad.

3. Whipping up the vinaigrette takes seconds. Combine all the ingredients to a small bowl and stir till smooth. Now pour over the Brussels sprouts salad and flip to bring together.

Epic Rosy Chicken Supreme Salad

What you need:

<u>For the chicken</u>:

- 1 stem lemon grass, pale section only, finely sliced
- 1 to 2 long red chili finely chopped with the seeds
- 2 to 3 garlic cloves, finely shredded
- Little nob of fresh ginger, peeled and finely shredded
- 1/2 lime rind grated
- Coconut oil for frying (About 3 tablespoons)
- 460g chicken mince, free range of course
- 2 1/2 tbsp fish sauce

- 1/2 bunch of coriander stems washed and finely chopped
- 1/2 lime (Juiced)
- 1 pinch of low sodium salt

For the salad:

- 1 handful of fresh mint or may be Thai basil if available
- 1 to 2 large carrot, peeled and grated
- 1/2 Spanish onion, thinly sliced
- 1/2 cup crushed roasted cashews or some sesame seeds
- 1/4 to 1/2 red cabbage, thinly sliced
- 1/2 to 1 bunch of fresh coriander leaves
- 2 tbsp green spring onion, sliced

For the dressing:

- 1 small red chili, finely shredded
- 3 tbsp lime juice
- 2 to 2 1/2 tbsp olive oil
- 1 to 2 tbsp fish sauce

What to do:

1. Once you've prepared all your ingredients for the chicken, heatup 1 tbsp of coconut oil in a large frying pan.

2. Throw in lemongrass, garlic, chili, coriander stems and ginger and stirfry for about a minute till fragrant.

3. Now you should add chicken mince and lime zest. Whisk

and break apart the mince with a wooden mixing spoon until they are separated into small chunks.

4. The meat will now be changing to white color.

5. Combine fish sauce and lime juice. Stir through and cook for a few minutes. Overall cooking time for the chicken should be about 10 to 15 minutes.

6. Prepare the salad base by mixing onion grated carrot, sliced red cabbage, and fresh herbs.

7. Combinewhole dressing ingredients and flip through the salad.

8. Now serve cooked chicken mince with a topping of the dressed salad and top it up with roasted cashews, dried shallots, coconut flakes, and extra fresh herbs.

Great Macadamia Chicken Salad

What you need:

- 1/2 cup diced celery
- 1 to 2 teaspoon macadamia nut oil, or oil of choice
- 1 tablespoon lemon juice
- 1 lb organic chicken breast
- 1/2 cup macadamia nuts, shredded
- few pinches of low sodium salt and pepper
- 2 tablespoons julienned basil
- 1 to 2 tbsp olive oil and 2 tsp rice vinegar

What to do:

1. Preheat oven to about 360 to 370 degree. Place chicken

breasts on a sheet tray, drizzle will oil and a pinch of low sodium pepper and salt.

2. Bake for about 30 to 40 minutes until cooked through.

3. Remove from oven and let it cool.

4. In a large bowl shred chicken.

5. Combine dressing, nuts, celery, basil, and a pinch of low sodium pepper and salt.

6. Lightly whisk till combined.

7. Time to party!

Awesometurkey Salad

What you need:

<u>For the Turkey:</u>

- Low sodium salt and pepper, to taste
- 1 tablespoon olive oil
- 1 to 2 pound boneless turkey breasts

<u>For the Salsa:</u>

- Juice of 1 lime
- 1/2 to 1 red onion, cut into large chunks
- low sodium salt and pepper, to taste
- 1 to 1 large tomato(Quartered)
- 1 small bunch of cilantro leaves

- 1 garlic clove(Peeled)

What to do:

1. First of all, preheat oven to about 380 to 390 F.
2. Bake turkey breasts dipped in olive oil on a baking sheet for about 40 to 45 minutes, till there is no longer pink in the center.
3. While baking, you should add all salsa to a food processor and pulse using the chopping blade till finely shredded. Shift the salsa to a large bowl and clean out the food processor. You will be using it to shred the turkey.
4. If you don't have a food processor, just dice the

tomato, pepper, onion, garlic and cilantro and combine to a bowl with the lime juice, low sodium pepper, and salt.

5. Remove turkey from the oven and allow it to cool. Once cooled enough to handle, cut every breast into 3 or maybe 4 smaller pieces and add to the food processor. Pulse using the chopping blade till shredded.

6. Combine turkey to bowl with salsa and blend well with a fork.

7. Refrigerate for at least 2 hours till turkey salad is chilled.

Extraordinary Red Bean Salad

What you need:

- 1 head chopped cabbage
- 1 to 1 1/2 chopped bell pepper
- Drizzle of olive oil
- Fifteen ounces of kidney beans
- 1 Minced clove of garlic
- 1 cup Feta cheese
- Drizzle of olive oil
- 1 tsp. Fresh parsley (Chopped)
- Drizzle of fresh lemon juice

What to do:

1. First, take the canned kidney beans and rinse well for a few minutes. In a large salad mixing bowl, you should combine the kidney beans,

onions, chopped cabbage, bell pepper and aminced clove of garlic. Tossthem together.

2. Then combine the parsley, lemon juice and drizzle olive oil and mix till coated. Top it up with feta cheese. Refrigerate for few hours and serve chilled.

King Bacon And Cherry Tomato Salad

What you need:

- 2 fresh cherry tomatoes now cut them into halves
- 5 slices of bacon
- Freshly ground black pepper to taste
- 2 fresh cherry tomatoes, cut them into halves
- Garlic salt to taste
- 1/2 cup crumbled fresh mozzarella or feta cheese
- Few fresh basil leaves

What to do:

1. Cook the slices of bacon until brown and then crumble

them and keep them in a bowl.

2. Now in a salad mixing bowl, combine the halved cherry tomatoes and fresh basil leaves along with crumbled fresh mozzarella or may be a feta cheese above them.

3. Now spread the crumbled bacon.

4. Top it up with pepper and garlic salt.

5. Serve immediately.

Exceptional Coconut Cream Dressing

What you need:

- 1 to 2 (0.7 ounces) packages dry Italian salad dressing mix
- 1/4 cup cider vinegar
- 1 to 2 (8.5 ounces) can cream of coconut

What to do:

1. In a small sized bowl, combine wholeof the ingredients then mix them well.
2. Serve, or maybe chill until ready so that you can serve.
3. You can refrigerate it for up to 1 week.

Yields: approximately 1 cup

Easy Macaroni Salad

What you need:

- Sugar, to taste
- 1/2 to 1 cup mayonnaise
- Salt to taste
- Freshly ground black pepper for seasoning
- 1 teaspoon. Dried mustard
- 1 stalk celery (Sliced)
- 1 cup cooked macaroni
- 1 red onion (Chopped)
- 1 to 2 teaspoon. sliced parsley
- 3 tbsp. Fresh sour cream
- Drizzle of cider vinegar

What to do:

1. Take a bowl and whisk mayonnaise along with the

fresh sour cream. Combine the dried mustard, drizzle of cider vinegar, salt, sugar and freshly ground black pepper to taste.

2. Mix well. Flip in the cooked macaroni and freshly sliced onion, celery and parsley and mix well.

3. Now serve immediately.

Fresh Chickpea And Salad

What you need:

- 1 tsp. chili powder
- Salt (In small quantity)
- 2 tomatoes (Chopped)
- 1 can chickpeas
- 2 to 3 cucumbers (Chopped)
- 2 to 3 red onions (Sliced)

What to do:

1. Boil the chickpeas in a pot till tender. Put in a mixing bowl with the tomatoes, red onions and cucumber pieces.
2. Blend everything together very well. Season with salt and chili powder and mix well.

3.   Now serve it instantly.

Green Pea Salad With Egg

What you need:

- 6 cherry tomatoes, now cut in halves
- 3 eggs
- Garlic powder to taste
- 1 to 2 tsp. fresh cilantro (Shredded)
- 2 cans fresh green peas
- 2 fresh onions (Sliced)
- 4 tablespoons. Fresh lemon juice
- Salt to taste

What to do:

1.   Mix the onions, peas, cherry tomatoes, and fresh cilantro. Now squeeze in fresh lemon

juice, combine few salt, and garlic powder.

2. Blend well. Boil the eggs to make some hard boiled eggs and now cut them into halves and mix to the salad bowl.

3. Now serve instantly.

Thanks for reading my book.

Made in the USA
Monee, IL
10 December 2023

48792690R00042